Table of contents:

Introduction: The Role Of Art And Creativity In Our Lives

Art and creativity have played a significant role in human history, helping us express ourselves, understand the world around us, and connect with one another. From the earliest cave paintings to the latest digital creations, art has been an essential part of our cultural and social evolution. In this book, we explore the ways in which art and creativity can help us thrive in today's world.

Creativity and art are often used interchangeably, but they are not the same thing. Creativity is the ability to use one's imagination to come up with new ideas, concepts, or ways of doing things. It is a fundamental human trait that allows us to innovate, problem-solve, and adapt to new situations.

On the other hand, art is the expression of creativity through a specific medium, such as painting, sculpture, music, dance, literature, and other mediums. Art involves a more intentional and structured use of creativity to produce something that is aesthetically pleasing, thought-provoking, or emotionally evocative, something that conveys an idea.

While art is one way of expressing creativity, not all creative activities are considered art. For example, coming up with a new business idea, designing a new product, or solving a complex math problem are all creative endeavours, but they are not typically considered art forms.

Furthermore, while some people may have a natural talent for art, creativity is a skill that can be developed and nurtured over time through practice, exploration, and experimentation. Ultimately, both creativity and art have the potential to enrich our lives and enhance our well-being in different ways.

At its core, creativity is the ability to think outside the box, to see things in a different way, and to approach problems from a fresh perspective. Art is the tangible expression of this creativity, and it can take many forms, from painting and sculpture to music, dance, and writing. Whether we are creating art ourselves or simply enjoying the art of others, it has the power to move us, inspire us, and help us connect with our inner selves and with each other.

In this book, we will explore how art and creativity can help us thrive in different areas of our lives, such as personal growth, relationships, work, and community engagement. We will also examine the science behind creativity, including the ways in which it affects our brains and our overall well-being.

Through stories, examples, and exercises, this book will provide you with practical tools and insights to help you tap into your own creativity, find inspiration in the world around you, and use art to enhance your life. Whether you are an artist, a creative professional, or simply someone who wants to bring more creativity into your daily life, this book is for you. Let's dive in and explore the wonderful world of art and creativity!

...But I am not an artist

You don't have to be an artist to practice art. Art is a form of creative expression that can be enjoyed by anyone, regardless of their skill level or background. In fact, many art therapy programs are specifically designed for individuals who have little or no experience with art. The focus is on the process of creating, rather than the end result. Engaging in art-making can be a fun and rewarding way to explore your emotions, relieve stress, and connect with others in a community setting. So, whether you're painting, drawing, sculpting, or working with mixed media, the benefits of practicing art are accessible to everyone.

Creative Activities Can Benefit Our Mental Health

Engaging in creative activities has been shown to have a positive impact on mental health. Studies have found that creative expression can help reduce stress, anxiety, and depression, while increasing positive emotions and overall well-being.

In a study published in the Journal of Positive Psychology in 2017, researchers found that people who engaged in creative activities such as writing, drawing, and playing music had a greater sense of well-being and experienced fewer negative emotions than those who did not engage in such activities.

The study, conducted by Tamlin S. Conner and Colin G. DeYoung at the University of Otago in Dunedin, New Zealand, involved 658 young adults who were asked to keep a daily diary of their creative activities and emotions over a 13-day period. The researchers found that engaging in creative activities was associated with positive mood, increased well-being, and lower levels of negative emotions. Specifically, they found that engaging in creative activities led to increased positive affect, decreased negative affect, and decreased depressive symptoms.

One reason for this is that creative activities allow us to focus our attention and enter a state of flow, which can promote feelings of happiness and fulfilment. Additionally, creative expression provides an outlet for emotions, allowing individuals to process difficult experiences and express themselves in a healthy way.

Research has also shown that engaging in creative activities can increase resilience and improve cognitive function. In one study published in the Journal of Aging and Health, older adults who participated in art programs experienced improved memory and cognitive function, as well as a reduced risk of depression.

Overall, incorporating creative activities into our lives can have numerous benefits for our mental health and well-being. From writing and drawing to playing music or dancing, there are countless ways to express our creativity and promote positive mental health.

There are many more creative activities that people can engage in, depending on their interests and skills. Some examples of other creative activities include:

Cooking or baking

Knitting, sewing, or other forms of textile art

Photography or videography

Acting or performing

Sculpting or pottery making

Graphic design or digital art.

These are just a few examples, and there are countless other creative activities that people can explore and enjoy.

Art Impacts Our Emotional Wellbeing

Art has been shown to have a significant impact on our emotional well-being. Engaging in artistic activities has been found to reduce stress, anxiety, and depression, while increasing positive emotions like joy, satisfaction, and self-expression. This is because art has the ability to connect us to our emotions in a unique and powerful way. It allows us to express feelings that may be difficult to put into words and to release negative emotions through creative expression.

Studies have found that art therapy can be particularly effective in treating individuals with mental health issues such as depression, anxiety, and post-traumatic stress disorder. Art therapy uses the creative process to help individuals explore their emotions and find new ways of coping with difficult feelings.

In addition to art therapy, simply engaging in creative activities like painting, drawing, writing, dancing, acting, etc., can have a positive impact on our emotional well-being. These activities can provide a sense of accomplishment and boost self-esteem, while also promoting relaxation and mindfulness.

Overall, the impact of art on our emotional well-being is significant and can be a valuable tool for promoting mental health and wellness.

A study published in the Journal of Affective Disorders found that art therapy was effective in reducing symptoms of depression and anxiety in adults who had experienced traumatic events.

A study conducted by the University of Kentucky found that art therapy was effective in reducing symptoms of post-traumatic stress disorder (PTSD) in veterans.

A study published in the Journal of the American Art Therapy Association found that art therapy was effective in reducing symptoms of anxiety in children with asthma.

A study conducted by the National Institutes of Health found that art therapy was effective in reducing symptoms of anxiety and depression in women with breast cancer.

Overall, these studies demonstrate the powerful impact that art can have on our emotional wellbeing and its potential as a therapeutic tool for treating mental health issues.

Creative Expression Can Help Process Trauma

Creative expression can be a powerful tool for processing trauma as it allows individuals to express and explore their emotions and experiences in a safe and non-judgmental way. Trauma can often be difficult to talk about or even fully understand, and this can lead to individuals feeling overwhelmed, isolated, and unable to move forward. Creative expression, whether through art, writing, music, dance, or other forms, can provide an outlet for these complex feelings and experiences.

There have been many studies that suggest that creative expression can help individuals process trauma. For example, a 2016 study published in the Journal of Traumatic Stress found that expressive writing, in which participants wrote about traumatic events, reduced symptoms of post-traumatic stress disorder (PTSD) and improved overall psychological functioning.

Similarly, a 2018 study published in the Journal of Affective Disorders found that engaging in creative activities such as music, art, and dance was associated with improved mental health outcomes in individuals with PTSD.

One of the ways a creative expression can help process trauma is by providing a sense of control. Trauma can make individuals feel powerless, and creative expression can give them agency over their experiences. It can allow them to tell their own story, rather than feeling like their trauma is defining them.

Additionally, creative expression can help individuals make sense of their experiences. Trauma can be confusing, and creative expression can provide a way to explore and understand the complex emotions and thoughts associated with it. It can also provide a way to identify and express previously unrecognized or suppressed emotions.

Another benefit of creative expression in processing trauma is that it can be a way to connect with others who have had similar experiences. Sharing creative work with others can foster a sense of community and support, and allow individuals to feel less alone in their experiences.

Finally, creative expression can be a form of self-care. Trauma can take a toll on both mental and physical health, and engaging in creative expression can be a way to promote healing and relaxation. It can also serve as a distraction from stressors or provide a sense of accomplishment and fulfilment.

There have also been studies that suggest that creative expression can help individuals cope with a variety of other mental health issues, including depression, anxiety, and substance abuse. Overall, while more research is needed in this area, the existing studies provide strong support for the idea that creative expression can be an effective tool for processing trauma and improving mental health outcomes.

Practicing Art In A Community Setting

Practicing art in a community setting can have numerous benefits for individuals and the community as a whole.

Firstly, creating art together in a community setting can foster a sense of connection and belonging among participants. This can be especially beneficial for individuals who may feel isolated or disconnected from their community, such as those experiencing social anxiety, depression, or grief.

Additionally, creating art in a group setting can provide a safe and supportive space for individuals to express themselves and explore their emotions. This can be particularly valuable for individuals who have experienced trauma or who may be struggling with mental health issues. Through art-making, individuals may be able to process difficult emotions in a healthy and constructive way, which can help promote healing and growth.

Participating in art-making in a community setting can also provide individuals with opportunities to learn new skills and techniques, as well as to share their own expertise with others. This can foster a sense of mastery and confidence in one's own abilities, which can have a positive impact on overall well-being.

Finally, practicing art in a community setting can have positive effects on the broader community as well. It can promote a sense of cultural vibrancy and diversity, and can be a powerful tool for social change and advocacy. Art can bring people together around shared values and goals, and can help to raise awareness and build empathy around issues such as social justice, environmental sustainability, and mental health.

Overall, practicing art in a community setting can be a powerful tool for fostering connection, healing, and growth, both for individuals and for the community as a whole.

there are many studies that have shown the benefits of practicing art in a community setting. Here are a few examples:

A study published in the Journal of Aging and Health found that older adults who participated in a community-based arts program had improved physical health, better cognitive functioning, and increased social engagement compared to those who did not participate.

A study published in the American Journal of Public Health found that community arts programs can improve mental health outcomes, including reducing symptoms of depression and anxiety.

A report by the National Endowment for the Arts found that community arts programs can foster social connections, build trust, and create a sense of belonging among participants.

Another study published in the Journal of Applied Arts and Health found that community arts programs can improve quality of life for individuals with chronic illnesses, including reducing symptoms and improving overall well-being.

Overall, there is a growing body of research that supports the benefits of practicing art in a community setting, including improved physical and mental health, increased social connections and sense of belonging, and improved quality of life.

The Connection Between Art And Mindfulness

Art can be a powerful tool for practicing mindfulness. Mindfulness involves focusing on the present moment and experiencing it fully without judgment or distraction. Engaging in art can help to achieve this state of mindfulness by encouraging focus on the process of creating rather than worrying about the end result. When creating art, we become fully engaged in the present moment, paying attention to the details of what we are making, and letting go of other concerns and worries.

In addition to helping us achieve mindfulness, art can also be a form of meditation in and of itself. The process of creating art can be calming and meditative, helping to reduce stress and anxiety. Studies have shown that engaging in creative activities like painting, drawing, or even colouring can lower cortisol levels (the stress hormone) and increase feelings of relaxation and calm.

Furthermore, art can be a form of self-expression that can help us better understand and manage our emotions. Through art, we can express feelings that may be difficult to put into words, providing an outlet for emotions that may be difficult to process otherwise. This can lead to a greater sense of self-awareness and emotional regulation, as well as a deeper connection to ourselves and our emotions.

One famous example of utilizing art and creativity as a tool to express and process difficult emotions is the author and poet Maya Angelou. Angelou used writing as a form of therapy and credited it with helping her overcome traumatic experiences in her life. In her memoir "I Know Why the Caged Bird Sings," Angelou writes about how writing helped her process and make sense of her experiences, saying, "I wrote myself into existence."

Angelou's writing often involved free association and stream-of-consciousness techniques, allowing her to explore her thoughts and emotions in a raw and unfiltered way. This type of writing can be particularly helpful for processing trauma, as it allows the person to access and express emotions that may be difficult to articulate in more structured forms of writing.

Many other writers and artists have also used associative writing as a tool for personal growth and healing. For example, James Pennebaker, a professor of psychology at the University of Texas, has conducted extensive research on the therapeutic benefits of expressive writing, including free association and other techniques.

James Pennebaker is a social psychologist and researcher who has extensively studied the effects of writing on emotional and physical health. In the 1980s, he conducted a landmark study that found a connection between writing and improved immune system functioning. In the study, college students were asked to write about their deepest thoughts and emotions surrounding a traumatic event for 20 minutes a day for four consecutive days. The control group was asked to write about a non-emotional topic, such as their daily activities. The results showed that the students who wrote about their trauma had improved immune system functioning compared to the control group.

Pennebaker's research has also shown that expressive writing can have positive effects on mental health. In a study published in the Journal of Clinical Psychology, participants with depression were randomly assigned to either write about their deepest thoughts and emotions surrounding their traumatic experiences or to write about a neutral topic for 20 minutes a day for three consecutive days. The results showed that the expressive writing group had significant reductions in depressive symptoms compared to the control group.

Furthermore, Pennebaker has found that the benefits of expressive writing are not limited to just emotional and physical health. In a study published in the Journal of Personality and Social Psychology, participants who wrote about their deepest thoughts and emotions surrounding a traumatic event for 20 minutes a day for four consecutive days reported better academic performance in the following months compared to a control group.

Pennebaker's research provides compelling evidence for the power of expressive writing in promoting emotional, physical, and academic well-being.

Another example is Natalie Goldberg, a writer and teacher who developed a method called "writing practice" as a form of mindfulness practice. Goldberg's method involves setting a timer for a certain amount of time (usually 10-15 minutes) and writing continuously without stopping, editing, or worrying about grammar or punctuation. The goal is to let the words flow without judgment or self-censorship, and to simply be present with the act of writing.

Goldberg has written several books on writing practice, including "Writing Down the Bones" and "Wild Mind." In these books, she emphasizes the importance of mindfulness in writing, and how writing can be a tool for self-discovery and healing.

Goldberg's approach to writing and mindfulness has inspired many writers and artists to use writing as a form of meditation and self-expression. Her method is accessible to anyone, regardless of their level of writing experience or skill, and can be a powerful tool for developing mindfulness and self-awareness.

Overall, practicing art can be a powerful tool for achieving mindfulness, reducing stress and anxiety, and improving emotional wellbeing.

Creativity As A Tool For Personal Growth And Self-Discovery

Creativity has long been recognized as a powerful tool for personal growth and self-discovery.

Personal growth and self-discovery allow us to become more self-aware and conscious of our thoughts, emotions, and behaviours. When we take the time to reflect on ourselves and explore our inner worlds, we can gain a better understanding of our strengths, weaknesses, values, and goals. This knowledge can help us make better decisions and choices that align with our authentic selves, leading to a more fulfilling and meaningful life.

Personal growth and self-discovery can also help us build resilience, improve our relationships with others, and increase our capacity for empathy and compassion. This process is a lifelong journey that can lead to greater self-acceptance, self-love, and a deeper sense of purpose and meaning.

Engaging in creative activities can provide individuals with an opportunity to explore and express their thoughts, emotions, and experiences in a non-judgmental and cathartic way. The process of creating art or writing can be therapeutic and can help individuals develop a deeper understanding of themselves and their world.

One way that creativity can aid in personal growth is by promoting self-reflection. Through the act of creating, individuals can gain a better understanding of their own emotions, beliefs, and values. This self-awareness can lead to personal growth and an increased sense of authenticity and purpose.

Additionally, engaging in creative activities can foster a sense of curiosity and experimentation. This mindset can translate to other areas of life, encouraging individuals to try new things and take risks. It can also foster resilience and problem-solving skills as individuals learn to navigate challenges and setbacks in the creative process.

Ultimately, creativity can provide individuals with a sense of fulfilment and meaning in their lives. Whether it's through creating art, writing, or engaging in other creative endeavours, individuals can use their creativity as a tool for personal growth and self-discovery.

The Relationship Between Creativity And Innovation

Creativity and innovation are closely linked, with creativity being the foundation upon which innovation is built. Creativity is the ability to come up with original and useful ideas, while innovation is the

implementation of those ideas into practice.
Without creativity, there would be no new
ideas to innovate upon.

Innovation is crucial for progress, both in
the arts and in other fields such as
technology, business, and science. Creative
individuals and teams are often responsible
for breakthroughs that change the way we
think and interact with the world around us.
Innovations can lead to new products,
services, and processes that can have a
profound impact on society and the
economy.

Creativity is also essential for businesses
and organizations that want to stay
competitive and adapt to changing markets
and trends. Companies that foster a culture
of creativity and innovation are often more
successful in identifying new opportunities
and staying ahead of the curve.

Moreover, creativity and innovation can also
enhance personal growth and development.
By challenging ourselves to think in new
and innovative ways, we can broaden our
perspectives and gain new insights into
ourselves and the world around us. This can

lead to a greater sense of purpose and fulfilment in our personal and professional lives.

Einstein is famously quoted as saying, "Creativity is intelligence having fun." This quote highlights the idea that creativity is not just about coming up with something new or unique, but it's also about using one's intelligence to approach problems and tasks in a different way, while also finding joy in the process.

Einstein's quote suggests that creativity and intelligence are not mutually exclusive, and that the most successful innovators and problem solvers are those who can harness both creativity and intelligence in their work.

...But I don't know what to make

While creativity can be a powerful tool for personal growth and innovation, it's not always a smooth and easy process. There can be many obstacles and challenges that come up when trying to be creative. Some common hurdles include self-doubt, fear of failure or rejection, lack of inspiration or motivation, perfectionism, and creative blocks.

Overcoming these hurdles requires persistence, resilience, and a willingness to experiment and take risks. It's important to remember that creativity is not a linear process, and setbacks and challenges are an inevitable part of the journey. By staying open to new possibilities, cultivating a positive mindset, and seeking support from others, people can overcome these obstacles and tap into their creative potential.

There are several common problems that people might face when trying to be creative. These might include:

Self-doubt

Fear of failure

Lack of inspiration

Perfectionism

Lack of time

Lack of resources

Creative blocks

It's important to remember that everyone faces challenges when it comes to being creative, and there is no one-size-fits-all solution. However, by recognizing these common problems and actively working to overcome them, individuals can unlock their creative potential and find new ways to express themselves.

The Creative Choices: Learning Through Decisions

In the tapestry of human experience, creativity often serves as the vibrant thread that weaves through the mundane, transforming the ordinary into the extraordinary. Creativity is not merely an abstract concept reserved for artists and dreamers; it is a dynamic force that pushes individuals to make choices, guiding them through a landscape of possibilities and uncertainties.

Unlike decisions made under life-and-death circumstances, creative choices are typically low-stakes, reducing stress and providing a fertile ground for learning and growth. This chapter delves into how creativity influences decision-making and how the relatively low-stress environment of creative choices fosters a valuable skill set for navigating life's myriad challenges.

The nature of creative choices:

Creative choices are decisions made in the pursuit of innovation, expression, and problem-solving. They are inherently experimental and often involve exploring uncharted territories. Whether it's choosing a colour palette for a painting, crafting a storyline for a novel, or devising a novel solution to a technical problem, these choices require an imaginative leap. The nature of these decisions is such that there are no absolute right or wrong answers, but rather a spectrum of possibilities each offering different outcomes.

Creativity pushes individuals to make a plethora of choices, each one a step in the journey of innovation and expression. The relatively low-stress environment of these decisions fosters a unique opportunity for growth, allowing individuals to develop essential decision-making skills without the pressure of dire consequences.

By engaging in creative activities, people learn to navigate uncertainty, solve problems, think critically, and build confidence—skills that are invaluable in both personal and professional realms. Ultimately, the practice of making creative choices teaches individuals not just how to make decisions, but how to embrace the process of decision-making as a vital and enriching aspect of life.

Exploration Over Fear - Because creative decisions are not tied to survival, individuals are more willing to explore and take risks. This reduces the fear of failure, encouraging experimentation and fostering an environment where mistakes are seen as learning opportunities rather than setbacks.

Reducing Stress Through Creative Freedom - One of the key aspects of creative decision-making is the relative absence of high stakes. Unlike decisions that directly impact one's survival or well-being, creative choices typically do not carry severe consequences. This alleviation of pressure allows individuals to engage more deeply with the process and focus on the joy of creation itself.

Safe Space for Experimentation - The creative process often provides a safe space to try new things without fear of significant repercussions. This can be incredibly liberating and conducive to innovation. For instance, a writer might draft several versions of a story to explore different narrative directions, or a software developer might test various coding solutions to find the most efficient one.

- Iterative Learning - Because the stakes are lower, individuals can afford to iterate on their ideas. This iterative process—trying, failing, learning, and trying again—cultivates resilience and adaptability.

Over time, individuals become more comfortable with uncertainty and ambiguity, essential components of both creative and practical problem-solving.

- Developing Decision-Making Skills - Engaging in creative activities necessitates a continuous series of choices. These choices, while often small, accumulate to shape larger outcomes. Through this process, individuals develop and refine their decision-making skills in a manner that is both enjoyable and instructive.
- Enhanced Problem-Solving Abilities - Creativity often involves identifying problems and generating novel solutions. For example, a designer working on a new product must consider functionality, aesthetics, and user experience, balancing these factors to create a cohesive whole. This problem-solving practice translates to other areas of life, where individuals can

apply creative thinking to tackle challenges.

Critical Thinking - Making creative choices requires evaluating options, considering various perspectives, and anticipating potential outcomes. This cultivates critical thinking skills, as individuals learn to weigh evidence, assess risks, and make informed decisions.

Confidence Building - Successfully navigating creative decisions builds confidence. Each small victory reinforces the belief in one's ability to make good choices, fostering a sense of agency and self-efficacy. This growing confidence can spill over into other domains, encouraging individuals to take on more significant challenges.

The role of feedback:

Feedback plays a crucial role in the creative decision-making process. Constructive criticism and praise from peers, mentors, or audiences provide valuable insights that help individuals refine their choices and improve their work.

- Learning from Others - Receiving feedback allows individuals to see their work from different perspectives. This can illuminate blind spots and introduce new ideas, enriching the creative process and enhancing decision-making skills.
- Adjusting and Improving - Feedback encourages adjustments and improvements. For instance, an artist might tweak a composition based on viewers' reactions, or a musician might alter a piece after hearing audience feedback. This adaptability is a critical component of effective decision-making.

Transferring skills to real-world situations:

The decision-making skills honed through creative endeavours are not confined to artistic or innovative pursuits. They are transferable to various aspects of life, including personal relationships, professional environments, and everyday problem-solving.

Personal Growth:

Creative decision-making fosters personal growth by encouraging introspection, self-expression, and emotional intelligence. Understanding one's preferences and values through creative choices helps in making more aligned and authentic life decisions.

Professional Success:

In the workplace, the ability to think creatively and make informed decisions is highly valued. Employees who can approach problems with innovative solutions and adapt to changing circumstances are more likely to thrive and advance in their careers.

Everyday Problem-Solving:

Whether managing household tasks, planning a trip, or resolving conflicts, the decision-making skills developed through creativity can make everyday life smoother and more enjoyable.

A Note On Creativity And Employment Opportunities

Creativity is becoming an increasingly important trait that employers are seeking in potential employees. This is because creativity is seen as a key driver of innovation and success in today's rapidly changing business world. In fact, a survey conducted by Adobe found that 78% of respondents believe that creativity is important to economic growth.

Employers are looking for individuals who can think outside the box, come up with novel solutions to problems, and generate new ideas that can help their company stay ahead of the competition. Creative individuals are often able to see things from a different perspective, which allows them to identify opportunities that others may miss. They are also more adaptable and open to change, which is essential in an ever-evolving business landscape.

Furthermore, creative individuals are often excellent communicators and collaborators. They are able to convey their ideas effectively and work well with others to bring those ideas to life. This is particularly important in team-based environments where innovation and collaboration are critical to success.

Overall, creativity is seen as a valuable asset in today's workplace, and employers are actively seeking individuals who possess this trait. By demonstrating your creativity through your work, projects, and other endeavours, you can increase your value to potential employers and position yourself for success in your career.

Overcoming Self-Doubt In Creativity

Self-doubt is a common companion on the creative journey. It whispers in our ears that our work is not good enough, that we lack talent, or that our ideas are unworthy. Overcoming self-doubt is essential for unlocking our full creative potential. This chapter explores the roots of self-doubt, its impact on creativity, and practical strategies to conquer it.

Understanding Self-Doubt

Self-doubt arises from various sources: past experiences, societal expectations, and our inner critic. It can manifest as perfectionism, fear of failure, or impostor syndrome. Understanding its origins is the first step in overcoming it.

Perfectionism: The belief that only flawless work is valuable. This can paralyze creativity, as the fear of making mistakes prevents experimentation and growth.

Fear of Failure: The dread of not meeting expectations, whether our own or others'. This fear can lead to procrastination or abandoning projects altogether.

Impostor Syndrome: The feeling that one's achievements are due to luck rather than skill, leading to a persistent sense of inadequacy.

The Impact of Self-Doubt on Creativity

Self-doubt can stifle creativity, limiting our willingness to take risks and explore new ideas. It can cause creative blocks, sap motivation, and lead to a cycle of negative thinking. However, recognizing its impact empowers us to take action against it.

Creative Blocks: Self-doubt can halt the creative process, making it difficult to start or complete projects.

Reduced Innovation: Fear of failure and perfectionism can inhibit the exploration of unconventional ideas, stifling innovation.

Decreased Motivation: Persistent self-doubt can lead to feelings of hopelessness and reduce the drive to create.

Strategies to Overcome Self-Doubt

Overcoming self-doubt requires a combination of mindset shifts, practical strategies, and supportive practices. Here are several approaches to help reclaim your creative confidence.

embrace Imperfection

Perfection is an unattainable standard that can cripple creativity. Embracing imperfection allows for growth and experimentation.

Practice Makes Progress: Focus on progress rather than perfection. Each creative endeavour is an opportunity to learn and improve.

Celabrate Mistakes☐ View mistakes as valuable learning experiences. They are often stepping stones to greater creativity and innovation.

Challenge Negative Thoughts

Self-doubt is fuelled by negative thinking. Challenging and reframing these thoughts can diminish their power.

Identify the Inner Critic: Recognize the negative voice in your mind. Understanding its patterns can help you counter its influence.

Reframe Negative Thoughts: Replace negative thoughts with positive affirmations. For example, instead of thinking "I'm not talented enough," affirm "I am capable and improving every day."

Set Realistic Goals

Setting achievable goals can build confidence and provide a sense of accomplishment.

Break Down Projects: Divide large projects into smaller, manageable tasks. This makes the creative process less overwhelming and allows for incremental progress.

Celebrate Achievements: Acknowledge and celebrate each milestone. This reinforces a positive mindset and motivates continued effort.

Seek Feedback and Support

Constructive feedback and support from others can provide valuable perspective and encouragement. It can be scary at first to reveal your creations since they can feel very personal, but you will probably be surprised by how much positive response you'll get. That said, it's important to choose the right people to show your work to. If you know that a certain individual is generally negative and unsupportive, it might be best to find those who will be able to offer constructive, rather than destructive, criticism.

Find a Creative Community: Surround yourself with supportive individuals who understand the creative process. Join local art groups, online forums, or attend workshops.

Request Constructive Criticism: Seek feedback from trusted sources. Constructive criticism can help improve your work and build confidence in your abilities.

Cultivate a Growth Mindset

Adopting a growth mindset—believing that abilities can be developed through dedication and hard work—can transform how you approach creativity.

Embrace Challenges: View challenges as opportunities to grow rather than obstacles to fear.

Learn from Others: Study the work and journeys of other creatives. Understanding their struggles and triumphs can inspire and motivate you.

Practice Mindfulness and Self-Compassion

Mindfulness and self-compassion can help manage the emotional aspects of self-doubt.

Mindfulness Practices: Engage in mindfulness activities such as meditation, journaling, or deep breathing. These practices can help you stay present and reduce anxiety.

Self-Compassion: Treat yourself with the same kindness and understanding that you would offer a friend. Recognize that self-doubt is a common human experience and be gentle with yourself.

Overcoming self-doubt is an ongoing process. It requires patience, persistence, and a willingness to challenge deeply ingrained beliefs. By embracing imperfection, challenging negative thoughts, setting realistic goals, seeking feedback, cultivating a growth mindset, and practicing mindfulness and self-compassion, you can reclaim your creative confidence.

Remember, every creative journey is unique. The presence of self-doubt does not diminish your talent or potential. It is merely a hurdle to be overcome. By taking proactive steps to address self-doubt, you open the door to greater creativity, innovation, and personal fulfilment. Embrace your creative potential and allow yourself the freedom to explore, experiment, and grow. The world needs your unique voice and vision.

Conclusion: Embracing Art And Creativity For A Thriving Life

As we journey through life, art and creativity stand as beacons of self-expression, healing, and growth. In "How Art and Creativity Help Us Thrive," we have explored the profound impact that engaging in creative activities can have on our mental, emotional, and social well-being. This conclusive chapter synthesizes the insights from previous chapters, reinforcing the transformative power of creativity and art in our lives.

The Integral Role of Art and Creativity

From the outset, we established that art and creativity are not mere pastimes but vital elements of human existence. They enrich our daily lives, offering avenues for self-expression and connection with others. As we engage with creative activities, we tap into a fundamental aspect of our humanity, cultivating a deeper understanding of ourselves and the world around us.

Mental Health Benefits

Engaging in creative activities has been shown to significantly benefit mental health. Whether through painting, writing, music, dance, cooking, carpentering, coding, and more, the act of creating can reduce stress, alleviate anxiety, and combat depression. It provides a therapeutic outlet, allowing individuals to express complex emotions and experiences that might be difficult to articulate otherwise.

Emotional Wellbeing

Art has a profound impact on our emotional wellbeing. Creative expression helps us navigate the spectrum of human emotions, fostering resilience and emotional intelligence. It allows us to process and release emotions in a healthy manner, leading to a more balanced and fulfilled life.

Healing Trauma Through Art

Creative expression is a powerful tool for processing trauma. By externalizing painful experiences through art, individuals can begin to heal and make sense of their past. Art therapy has been recognized for its effectiveness in helping people work through trauma, offering a safe space for expression and reflection.

The Power of Community Art

Practicing art in a community setting amplifies its benefits. Shared creative experiences foster social connections, build supportive networks, and create a sense of belonging. Community art projects can bridge cultural divides, promote understanding, and strengthen communal bonds.

Art and Mindfulness

There is a profound connection between art and mindfulness. Engaging in creative activities requires a focused presence, immersing individuals in the moment and providing a reprieve from the constant distractions of daily life. This mindful engagement enhances self-awareness and promotes mental clarity.

Personal Growth and Self-Discovery

Creativity is a catalyst for personal growth and self-discovery. Through the creative process, individuals explore their identities, values, and aspirations. It encourages introspection and self-reflection, leading to greater self-knowledge and personal development.

Creativity and Innovation

The relationship between creativity and innovation is undeniable. Creative thinking drives innovation, fostering new ideas and solutions. In both personal and professional contexts, the ability to think creatively is invaluable, leading to breakthroughs and advancements.

<u>Learning Through Creative Choices</u>

As discussed in "The Creative Choices: Learning through Decisions," engaging in creative activities teaches us to navigate uncertainty and make decisions with confidence. The relatively low-stress environment of creative choices allows for experimentation and learning, building decision-making skills that are transferable to other areas of life.

Final Thoughts

In conclusion, art and creativity are essential for a thriving life. They nurture our mental and emotional health, facilitate healing, foster community, enhance mindfulness, drive personal growth, and fuel innovation. By embracing creativity, we open ourselves to a richer, more fulfilling existence. Let us continue to prioritize and cultivate art and creativity in our lives, reaping the myriad benefits they offer and inspiring others to do the same.

Through this book, we hope to have illuminated the profound impact of art and creativity, encouraging you to explore and integrate these practices into your own life. As you embark on your creative journey, remember that every stroke of the brush, every word written, and every note played contributes to your well-being and helps you thrive.

Resources

Here's a list of resources for those looking to explore and enhance their creativity through various forms of artistic expression and creative development:

<u>Books on Creativity and Art</u>

"The Artist's Way" by Julia Cameron - A seminal book on creativity, offering exercises and tools for unlocking artistic potential.

"Big Magic: Creative Living Beyond Fear" by Elizabeth Gilbert - Insights and inspiration for living a creative life without fear.

"Steal Like an Artist" by Austin Kleon - Practical advice on how to find inspiration and be more creative.

"Drawing on the Right Side of the Brain" by Betty Edwards - Techniques to improve drawing skills and unlock creative potential.

"The War of Art" by Steven Pressfield - A guide to overcoming creative blocks and inner resistance.

"Creative Confidence" by Tom Kelley and David Kelley - Encouraging creativity in everyday life and work.

"Flow: The Psychology of Optimal Experience" by Mihaly Csikszentmihalyi - Understanding the state of flow and its importance in creative activities.

<u>Online Courses and Platforms</u>

Coursera - Offers courses on creativity, art, and design from top universities.

Udemy - A variety of courses on artistic techniques, creative writing, and more.

Skillshare - Classes on a wide range of creative skills, including illustration, photography, and music.

MasterClass - Lessons from renowned artists, writers, musicians, and creators.

Khan Academy - Free courses on art history and techniques.

- Many community centres offer art classes and creative workshops. Check local listings.
- Many cities have adult education programs with classes in art, music, and creative writing.
- Continuing education programs at art schools and universities often offer short courses and workshops.

These resources provide some of the variety of ways to explore and develop creativity, from learning new artistic skills to connecting with other creatives and finding inspiration for your own projects.

There are also many online groups that support creativity and might help you get your juices flowing, such as:

Happenstantial Art

Liminal Spaces

Clouds Around The World

Peeling Paint Appreciation Society

Fractalgasm

Ninja Writers

… All these happen to be on Facebook, but there are many more creative communities and resources available across the online multiverse. These include free photo editing software like Canva and Photopea, random word/sentence and prompt generators, and a plethora of other tools. Additionally, there are numerous online groups and forums on various social media platforms and websites that can inspire and support your creative journey. Some of these include:

Reddit Communities:

r/Art - A place to share and discover new art and get feedback.

r/WritingPrompts - Offers a wide range of writing prompts to spark creativity.

r/Photography - A community for photographers to share their work and gain inspiration.

Instagram:

@art_spotlight - Features artists from around the world and their work.

@writersofig - A community for writers to share their pieces and connect with other writers.

@creativephotography - Showcases creative photography from various photographers.

Pinterest:

Creative Inspiration Boards - Search for boards dedicated to various forms of art, DIY projects, and creative ideas.

Writing Prompts and Ideas - Explore boards with writing prompts and tips for writers.

Tumblr:

Art and Aesthetic Blogs - Follow blogs that share beautiful art and creative ideas.

Writing Challenge Blogs - Participate in writing challenges and prompts to keep your creativity flowing.

Discord:

Creative Corner - A server for artists, writers, and creators to share their work and collaborate.

Writers' Haven - A supportive community for writers to discuss ideas and improve their craft.

Websites and Forums:

DeviantArt - An online community where artists can share their work, get feedback, and connect with other artists.

Behance - A platform for showcasing and discovering creative work across various fields.

Wattpad - A community for writers to share their stories and connect with readers.

The Critique Circle - A forum where writers can get constructive feedback on their work.

By exploring these resources and joining these communities, you can find endless inspiration, gain valuable feedback, and connect with fellow creatives who share your passion.